12 ATHLETES
WITH DISABILITIES

by Joanne Mattern

12

STORY LIBRARY

MORE TO EXPLORE

www.12StoryLibrary.com

12-Story Library is an imprint of Bookstaves.

Photographs ©: Manny Flores/Cal Sport Media/Associated Press, cover, 1; PHOTOMDP/ Shutterstock.com, 4; Alextype/Shutterstock.com, 5; Henk Lindeboom/Anefo/CC3.0, 6; Science History Images/Alamy, 7; David P. Stein/YouTube, 8; David P. Stein/YouTube, 9; Heath Campanaro/CC3.0, 10; Mark Davidson/Alamy, 11; Clarke Henry/CC2.0, 12; Clarke Henry/CC2.0, 13; Save the Children Hong Kong/YouTube, 14; Save the Children Hong Kong/ YouTube, 15; JT Lewis/YouTube, 16; JT Lewis/YouTube, 17; Neal Simpson/PA Images/Alamy, 19; Prime Minister's Office, Government of India/GODL-India, 20; Muhammad Haseeb/ YouTube, 21; Down Syndrome Association of Central Texas/YouTube, 22; Larry D. Moore/ CC3.0, 23; Carolyn Kaster/Associated Press, 24; Larry Goren/Four Seam Images/Associated Press, 25; Diego Barbieri/Shutterstock.com, 26; Andy Rogers/CC2.0, 27; riopatuca/ Shutterstock.com, 28; Jaren Jai Wicklund/Shutterstock.com, 29

ISBN
9781632357526 (hardcover)
9781632358615 (paperback)
9781645820369 (ebook)

Library of Congress Control Number: 2019938642

Printed in the United States of America
October 2019

About the Cover
Oz Sanchez in 2012.

Access free, up-to-date content on this topic plus a full digital version of this book. Scan the QR code on page 31 or use your school's login at 12StoryLibrary.com.

Table of Contents

Alex Zanardi: Racing Champion

Alex Zanardi was a race car driver who could do almost anything on the track. He had been a Formula One driver in Italy. But his career really took off when he came to the United States. In 1995, he joined Championship Auto Racing Teams, or CART. He earned 14 first place finishes. He also won the North American CART Championships in 1997 and 1998.

In 2001, tragedy struck. Zanardi crashed into oncoming traffic during a race. The crash cut off both of his legs.

Zanardi was determined to keep racing. Just two years later, he was back on the racetrack. He wore specially designed prosthetic legs and used hand controls. In his first race after his crash, he finished in seventh place.

Zanardi decided to try something new. He started hand cycling. A hand cycle is a vehicle that looks like a bicycle, but it's powered by the rider's arms instead of legs. Zanardi won four gold medals at the 2012 and 2016 Paralympic Games.

Alex Zanardi is interviewed after a race in Italy in 2018.

Zanardi racing on his handbike in Rome in 2017.

DRIVING WITHOUT LEGS

How can a person without legs drive a car? Hand controls are the answer. In the past, these controls were often just long rods that extended from the gas and brake pedals to the driver's hands. Today, drivers can push or pull levers to accelerate or slow down. Different systems can be combined to meet each driver's needs.

2019

Year when Zanardi took part in the 24 Hours of Daytona race

- Teams of drivers race for 24 hours straight. Each driver takes a three-hour shift.
- Zanardi started endurance racing in 2015.
- He drove without prosthetic legs. Instead, he used special hand controls to drive the car.

5

Wilma Rudolph: From Polio to the Olympics

Wilma Rudolph in 1960.

Wilma Rudolph was born in Tennessee on June 23, 1940. The odds were against her from the start. Rudolph was premature. She weighed only four and a half pounds (2.0 kg). She was sick for most of her childhood and spent a lot of time in bed.

Then Rudolph got a crippling disease called polio. Doctors said she would never walk again. Her mother said she would. Rudolph decided to believe her mother and not the doctors.

There were 22 children in the Rudolph family, so someone was always around to help Wilma learn to walk. Her brothers and sisters rubbed her legs every day. When doctors gave her a brace for her left leg, she often took it off. Her brothers and sisters acted as lookouts so she wouldn't get in trouble. Her mother took time off from her job cleaning houses to drive her to therapy at a hospital every week.

By the time she was 11, Rudolph could walk normally. She started playing basketball. A few years later, she was the star of her high school team. One day, Ed Temple, the track coach at Tennessee State University, came to see her. Temple thought she would be a great sprinter. Rudolph started training with the college team. In 1956, at age 16, she qualified for the US Olympic Team.

Rudolph won a bronze medal at the 1956 Olympics. In 1960, she became the first American woman to win three gold medals in track and field at the same Olympics. People called her the fastest woman in the world.

Rudolph wins the women's 100 meter dash at the 1960 Summer Olympics in Rome.

1962
Year when Wilma Rudolph retired from track and field

- Rudolph went on to get a college degree and work in education.
- She started the Wilma Rudolph Foundation to encourage children to play sports.
- She inspired generations of track-and-field athletes.

Brent Sopel: Freedom on the Ice

Growing up in rural Canada during the 1980s taught Brent Sopel the meaning of hard work. But for him, the hardest work wasn't farm chores. It was school. When he tried to read, the words made no sense. Trying to do math gave him a headache.

Things were different on the ice. Every winter day, Sopel skated for hours on the homemade ice rink in his backyard. Everyone understood that skating and playing hockey were things he was good at.

Sopel's dream was to play professional hockey. In 1995, he started playing in hockey's minor leagues. He finally made it to the National Hockey League (NHL) in 1999. He played for 12 years. The highlight of his career was winning the Stanley Cup with the Chicago Blackhawks in 2010.

Something else happened in 2010 that changed Sopel's life. His six-year old daughter was diagnosed with dyslexia and dysgraphia. These are conditions that make reading and writing difficult. Sopel realized he had dyslexia and dysgraphia, too. He started the Brent Sopel Foundation to help support children with dyslexia. He doesn't want anyone to struggle the way he did when he wasn't playing hockey.

Brent Sopel in 2019.

143

Number of players chosen ahead of Brent Sopel in the 1995 NHL draft

- NHL teams thought Sopel was not smart. But he showed them that he had a natural ability to play the game.
- Sopel played minor league hockey with the Vancouver Canucks from 1995 to 1998.
- He played 1,000 games in North America.

THE STANLEY CUP

The Stanley Cup is named after Canada's Lord Frederick Arthur Stanley. The award is a huge silver cup, with the names of the winning team members engraved on the base. The first Stanley Cup game was held in 1894. The Cup has been awarded by the NHL almost every year since 1926.

Natalie du Toit: Swimming with One Leg

Natalie du Toit (center) at the Beijing Paralympics in 2008 after receiving her gold medal.

South African Natalie du Toit started swimming competitively in 1998, when she was 14. Three years later, she left swimming practice and climbed on her scooter to ride back to school. Suddenly, a car slammed into her. Her left leg was so badly damaged it had to be amputated at the knee.

Five months later, du Toit was back in the pool. At first, her missing leg meant she could only swim in circles. She learned to use her left arm to make up for her missing leg.

7.5

Distance in kilometers (4.66 miles) Natalie du Toit swam in an open water challenge in South Africa in 2009

- Du Toit won the race and beat the men's winner by more than a minute.
- Her time broke the women's world record for a 7.5 km (4.66 miles) open water swim.
- She faced chilly water temperatures and the chance of sharks during her swim.

In 2001, du Toit won two races for disabled swimmers at the Commonwealth Games, held in England. She also swam in an event for athletes without disabilities. This was the first time a disabled athlete had qualified to do that.

But du Toit didn't just want to swim with other disabled swimmers. She wanted to be an Olympian. After years of hard work, she qualified for the South African team at the 2008 Olympics. She also carried South Africa's flag at the Games. Du Toit placed 16th in the women's 10 km race (6.2 miles) and became the first disabled athlete to compete in the Olympics. She went on to win five gold medals at the Paralympic Games immediately following the Olympics.

THINK ABOUT IT

Do you think disabled athletes and those without disabilities should compete against each other? Why or why not?

Oz Sanchez: Overcoming Trouble

Oz Sanchez in 2007.

2009
Year when Sanchez was featured in a documentary called *Unbeaten*

- *Unbeaten* tells the story of several disabled athletes.
- The film focuses on the belief that nothing is impossible.
- Sanchez has the words "No Limits" tattooed on his chest.

Oz Sanchez was born in Los Angeles in 1975. From an early age, he was headed for trouble. By the time he graduatcd from high school, he was involved with drugs, gangs, and violence. He knew he had to change his life. In 1996, Sanchez joined the US Marines. The discipline and routine were exactly what he needed. For the next six years, he trained in diving, parachuting, and other specialties. In 2001, he decided to become a Navy SEAL.

While Sanchez was transferring from the Marines to the Navy, disaster struck. He was riding his motorcycle when he was involved in a hit-and-run accident. The accident injured his spinal cord and left him paralyzed.

Sanchez fought back with the same determination that got him through the Marines. This time, his focus was on athletics.

Sanchez took up the sport of hand cycling. By 2008, he was one of the top hand cyclists in the world. Sanchez competed in the Paralympic Games in 2008, 2012, and 2016. He won two gold, one silver, and three bronze medals.

The Paralympics aren't the only place where Sanchez shows his athletic abilities. He also competes in triathlons. These endurance events include running, cycling, and swimming, all in the same day. In his spare time, he trains at the gym and swims for fun.

Sanchez in the lead.

Yu Chui Yee:
One of the Best

Yu Chui Yee in 2016.

When Yu Chui Yee was 13, she lost most of her left leg to bone cancer. That didn't stop the Hong Kong teenager's love of sports.

At first, Yu was a swimmer. Then a friend told her there were a lot of cute boys in fencing. When Yu went to her first fencing lesson, she didn't see any cute boys, but she fell in love with the sport anyway.

Yu entered her first Paralympics in 2004, when she was 20 years old. She competed in wheelchair fencing and won four gold medals. She went on to win more in 2008, 2012, and 2016. She has won more Paralympic medals than any athlete in Hong Kong. Today she is considered one of the best Paralympians in the world.

Yu has won medals in other international competitions. She has also hosted a radio show, written for magazines, and founded her own fencing school. She wants to try scuba diving and paragliding. Meanwhile, she has started running.

Yu (right) competing in wheelchair fencing in 2016.

11

Medals Yu Chui Yee has won in the Paralympic Games

- Four years after her first wins at the 2004 Paralympics in Athens, Yu won a gold and a silver in Beijing.
- At the 2012 Games in London, she won two golds and a bronze.
- She won two silver medals at the 2016 Paralympics in Rio de Janeiro.

THE PARALYMPICS

After World War II, people wanted to find a way for disabled veterans to take part in sports. In 1948, the first competition for wheelchair athletes was held at the start of the London Olympics. This led to the first official Paralympic Games after the 1960 Rome Olympics. More than 400 athletes from 223 countries took part. Today, the Paralympics are always held after the Olympics in the same cities.

Tom Dempsey: Super Kicker

Tom Dempsey in 2018.

kick a football. He became a kicker during his days at college. He wore a special shoe that let him swing his leg and kick the ball with plenty of force.

Dempsey dreamed of playing in the National Football League (NFL). But no team would give him a chance. Finally, in 1969, he was signed by the New Orleans Saints. Dempsey had a great first season. He scored 99 points with a field goal in each of the first 12 games.

Then came the best moment of Dempsey's career. On November 8, 1970, the Saints trailed the Detroit Lions 17 to 16. With just two seconds left to play, Dempsey kicked a powerful field goal. The ball traveled 63 yards (57.6 m). The kick set an NFL record.

A few years later, the NFL decided that Dempsey's shoe gave him an unfair advantage. The league

Tom Dempsey's nickname was Stumpy. He was born in 1947 without toes on his right foot or fingers on his right hand. His missing toes didn't stop him from playing football. When he was growing up, Dempsey wrapped athletic tape around his right foot so he could

43

Years Dempsey held the record for the longest field goal

- The previous record was 56 yards (51 m), set in 1953.
- Matt Prater of the Denver Broncos broke Dempsey's record in 2013. He kicked a 64-yard (58.5 m) field goal.
- Three other players tied Dempsey's record in 1998, 2011, and 2012.

THINK ABOUT IT

Should disabled players be allowed to wear equipment that helps them? Why or why not?

passed the "Tom Dempsey Rule." This rule says players with artificial or missing limbs must wear normal kicking shoes.

Marla Runyan: Running Blind

Most athletes are good at one or two things. When it comes to track-and-field events, Marla Runyan is good at just about anything. This legally blind runner has achieved records in sprinting, middle- and long-distance running, and field events.

Runyan was born in 1969. When she was nine years old, she developed an eye disease that took away most of her sight. She could only see shapes and shadows. She could see things to the side, but she couldn't see anything straight ahead.

Runyan started running in college. She competed in many different events including the heptathlon, 200-meter dash, high jump, shot put, 100-meter hurdle, long jump, javelin throw, and 800-meter run.

Runyan won a gold medal at the 1992 Paralympic Games. She tried out for the US Olympic Team in 1996 but didn't qualify.

She competed in the Paralympics and won gold again.

Finally, in 2000, Runyan became the first legally blind American track-and-field athlete to qualify and compete for the US Olympic Team. She placed eighth in the 1,500-meter race.

5

Gold medals Marla Runyan won in the Paralympic Games

- Runyan set nine world records in Paralympic events.
- She hoped to make the 2008 Olympic Team but could not because of back problems.
- She and her husband are coaches at Northeastern University. She also teaches at the Perkins School for the Blind.

Marla Runyan (#3375) runs the 1,500-meter race at the 2000 Olympics in Sydney.

Runyan made the Olympic Team again in 2004.

In 2002, Runyan took fourth place in the New York City Marathon. She was the top American female to finish the race. Her time was 2 hours, 27 minutes, and 10 seconds. Runyan has also run marathons in other US cities.

Mariyappan Thangavelu: High Jump Hero

Mariyappan Thangavelu in 2016.

When Thangavelu was five years old, life got even harder. He was walking to school when he was run over by a bus. The accident damaged his right leg so badly it never grew. It stayed the size of a child's leg.

Thangavelu did not let his short leg stop him from playing sports. At first, he wanted to play volleyball. But that was too difficult with his disability. Then his high school PE teacher suggested he try the high jump. Thangavelu was

Life was never easy for Mariyappan Thangavelu. He was born into a poor family in India in 1995. When he was just a child, his father left the family. His mother supported herself and her children by selling vegetables in the market. She was determined that all of her children would go to school.

HELPING HIM JUMP

Thangavelu has said his short right leg makes him better at the high jump. He believes its size and shape give him better leverage when he pushes off. He thinks of that leg as his lucky charm.

Thangavelu (center) at the awards ceremony at the Paralympic Games in Rio in 2016.

hooked. He was spotted by a top coach and went to train with him.

In 2016, Thangavelu competed in the high jump at the Paralympic Games in Rio. He jumped 1.89 meters (6.2 feet) to win the gold medal.

In October 2018, Thangavelu represented India in the Asian Paralympic Games. He was India's flag bearer. Thangavelu won a bronze medal.

3

Number of Indians who have won gold medals at the Paralympics

- Thangavelu was the first Indian to win a gold medal in the high jump.
- This was India's first Paralympics gold medal in 12 years.
- An Indian film director is making a movie about Thangavelu's life.

Kayleigh Williamson: Marathon Queen

Kayleigh Williamson (center) celebrates her finish in 2019.

the Austin, Texas, half marathon in February 2017. Williamson has an intellectual disability called Down syndrome. People with Down syndrome can also have health issues, such as heart problems and poor muscle strength.

A marathon is a huge challenge for any athlete. Marathoners run just over 26 miles (42 km) without stopping. This is very hard on the body.

Instead of a full marathon, some runners compete in a half marathon. A half marathon is 13 miles (21 km). But it is still a feat of amazing endurance.

Kayleigh Williamson made history when she entered

The 27-year-old had taken part in Special Olympics basketball and swimming. But running was a new and different sport for her. She completed the course in 6 hours and 22 minutes. She was the first person with Down syndrome to run in and finish the Austin race. As Williamson neared the finish line, her mother, friends, and coaches ran with her.

Williamson finished the race again in 2018. In 2019, she completed the race in 4 hours and 8 minutes. That's a better time than many runners without disabilities are able to achieve.

AUSTINmarathon & HALF MARATHON®

Runners at the start of the marathon.

2013
Year when Kayleigh Williamson started running

- Running helped Williamson lose weight. It helped her sleep better at night. It also eased the symptoms of several medical conditions.
- Williamson's second-favorite sport is swimming.
- When she crossed the finish line in 2017, she did a victory dance.

THINK ABOUT IT

Why do people run marathons? What do they get out of doing something so challenging? Try to find out.

Jim Abbott: Different Can Be Better

Abbott loved baseball from an early age. He started playing Little League Baseball when he was 11 years old. Despite his disability, he developed into a talented pitcher. He would throw the ball with his left hand, then quickly shift his glove from his right arm onto his left hand so he could catch. The movement was so quick, Abbott rarely missed fielding anything that came his way.

Abbott played baseball in high school and college. In 1989, he joined the California Angels. Over the next ten years, he pitched for four different teams. The highlight of his career was pitching a no-hitter for the New York Yankees on September 4, 1993.

Jim Abbott in 2008.

Jim Abbott was born different, and he didn't like it. Abbott was born without his right hand. Growing up, he often hid his unfinished arm in his pocket.

After baseball, Abbott became a motivational speaker. He also continued working for children's charities.

$50,000

Signing bonus Jim Abbott turned down to go to college

- The signing bonus was offered by the Toronto Blue Jays.
- Abbott went to the University of Michigan and played baseball there for three years before leaving to join the major leagues.
- In 1988, Abbott was the first baseball player named Big Ten Conference Player of the Year.

A TOP AMATEUR ATHLETE

In 1987, Abbott pitched in the Pan American Games. He led the US team to a silver medal. He also won the Sullivan Award, which is given each year to the nation's best amateur athlete. In 1988, Abbott joined the US Olympic Team in Seoul, South Korea. He pitched a 5–3 complete game against Japan to win a gold medal. Abbott has called that game his biggest thrill in sports.

Abbot throws a pitch for the California Angels in 1995.

Im Dong-hyun:
On Target

Im Dong-hyun in 2011.

When this South Korean archer looks at a target, the colors look like drops of paint floating underwater. That's because Im Dong-hyun is legally blind. Im may have trouble reading an eye chart. But he has no trouble hitting the bull's-eye.

Im was born in 1986. A teacher suggested he start practicing archery. Im turned out

70
Distance in meters (230 feet) an archer stands from the target

- An archery target has rings of different colors.
- Rings get smaller as they move toward the center.
- Hitting the yellow center target is making a bull's-eye.

LEGALLY BLIND

Normal vision is 20/20. That means a person can see something 20 feet away that other people can also see at that distance. Someone who is legally blind has 20/200 vision or worse. The person can see something 20 feet away that other people can see from 200 feet away.

Im takes aim at the 2012 Olympics.

to be very good at the sport. In 2002, the 17-year-old made South Korea's national team. Two years later, he was at the Summer Olympics in Athens, Greece. Im made it to the individual quarterfinals before being eliminated. But he and his teammates won a gold medal in the team archery event.

In 2008, Im and his teammates won gold again. They took home a bronze medal at the 2012 Games. Im also set an individual world record at the

2012 Olympics but lost before the medal round.

Im says his many years of training and his intense focus have made him a champion. He brushes off comments about his eyesight. Im wants people to focus on his talent instead.

Learn More: Accessibility

If something is accessible, it is open to all. People with disabilities often feel like opportunities are closed to them. If they can't get into a building, they can't take part in what goes on inside. If they can't understand what's being said in a classroom, they can't learn.

Accessibility breaks down those walls and barriers. It seeks to make everything possible for people of all abilities. Accessibility might mean ramps or curb cuts in a sidewalk so a wheelchair user can get on or off it easily. It might mean automatic doors or an elevator so people can use all the facilities in a building, even if they have trouble walking. Accessibility can mean text-to-speech features on a computer or closed captioning on a film for people who have trouble hearing or speaking.

For disabled athletes, accessibility can mean the chance to compete with others. Sports have been shown to improve confidence and empower people of all abilities. Disabled athletes can benefit from the chance to be active and take part in sporting events.

In 1990, the United States government passed the Americans with Disabilities Act (ADA). It states that new construction had to be accessible to all. Older buildings also had to improve accessibility whenever possible. Great Britain, Australia, and other nations have also passed accessibility acts.

Accessibility is not just limited to physical buildings. Students who are struggling in school can be tested and programs developed to help them learn. Sports leagues such as Challenger Little League and BuddyBall pair special-needs players with non-special-needs children and teens so both can benefit and enjoy different sports.

Accessibility helps people achieve their goals. It makes our world more welcoming.

Glossary

amateur
A person who does something without getting paid.

amputated
Cut off.

competitively
In a way that tries to win.

draft
A procedure where teams select new players.

eliminated
Removed.

endurance
The ability to do something for a long time.

foundation
An organization that gives money to charity.

leverage
Power, like the advantage gained from using a lever.

prosthetic
An artificial limb.

qualify
To show the ability needed to take part in a competition.

sprinter
A person who races over a short distance.

therapy
Treatment to relieve or cure a medical problem.

Read More

Cohen, Stephanie. *Marla Runyan: In It for the Long Run.* New York: Macmillan/McGraw-Hill, 2009.

Johnson, Robin. *Paralympic Sports Events.* Winter Olympic Sports. New York: Crabtree Publishing Company, 2009.

Morganelli, Adrianna. *Wilma Rudolph: Track and Field Champion.* New York: Crabtree Publishing Company, 2017.

Zuckerman, Gregory. *Rising Above: How 11 Athletes Overcame Challenges in Their Youth to Become Stars.* New York: Philomel Books, 2016.

Visit 12StoryLibrary.com

Scan the code or use your school's login at **12StoryLibrary.com** for recent updates about this topic and a full digital version of this book. Enjoy free access to:

- Digital ebook
- Breaking news updates
- Live content feeds
- Videos, interactive maps, and graphics
- Additional web resources

Note to educators: Visit 12StoryLibrary.com/register to sign up for free premium website access. Enjoy live content plus a full digital version of every 12-Story Library book you own for every student at your school.

Index

About the Author

Joanne Mattern has been writing books for children for more than 25 years. She loves to write about sports and especially likes stories about inspiring athletes. Joanne lives in New York State with her family.